Info Guide

Attract customers fast
with Text Message
Marketing!

Send Advertisements,
Coupons and Limited
Time Offers that
pull in cusotmers.

I0473834

Everything You <u>MUST Know</u>
Before Using
Text Message Marketing!

Duke Morris

C y C o n   C o n s u l t i n g

Table of Contents

Text Message Marketing

Info Guide

Attract customers fast with Text Message Marketing!

Send Advertisements, Coupons and Limited Time Offers that pull in cusotmers.

Everything You **MUST** Know
Before Using
Text Message Marketing!

Everything You Must Know Before Using
Text Message Marketing

Copyright © 2012 Duke Morris

Published by CyCon Consulting, LLC

ISBN-13: 978-1475200874

ISBN-10: 10-1475200870

Printed in the United States of America

For more information, visit:
www.cyconsocialmedia.com

LEGAL NOTICES

What is Text Message Marketing?

If you're a small business owner and haven't yet heard of text message marketing, then you're missing out on a huge advertising opportunity.

Text message marketing, also known as Mobile Marketing, SMS Marketing or *short message marketing,* is the latest form of Internet and mobile advertising and it's quickly becoming extremely popular.

There are many advantages to text message marketing and the idea behind it and finding out how to get started, is all very straightforward and fairly simple. I intentionally avoid term easy, because that depends on complexities of your campaigns, which you can make as easy or as sophisticated as you wish..

Text message marketing works very directly and candidly. You create an advertisement and then broadcast it to just about anyone who has a cell phone with text messaging capabilities, which is just about all cell phones in use today.

How you get that ad out to those cell phones is up to you; you can hire a company that already has access to one or several subscriber lists, or you can create a subscriber list yourself, and distribute your own text message ads whenever you want.

 When your ad goes out, it is sent to each phone and every person on your subscriber list. And boom! They all have just received your ad campaign.

Although this guide will get into greater detail about each step later, it really is that simple. Once you've sent out your first text messaging ad and are ready to send another, just do it all over again.

And it can be so effective that you might find this new form of advertising quickly become your company's main form of advertising.

Benefits of Text Message Marketing

There's a reason why text message marketing is quickly taking over the advertising world by storm – and that's because there's no reason *not* to. Big corporations like McDonald's, Dunkin' Donuts, and Rogers are just a few that have already started taking advantage of the many benefits of this form of advertising.

But it's not just the big names that can take part, this form of marketing is perfect for small and very small businesses too.

Probably the biggest advantage to text message marketing is that your message, whatever it contains, reaches a mass amount of people at one time. This beats out even television and radio advertising, where you have to count on your target audience to be listening or watching at the time your ad is on the air.

Even bulletin boards, with their huge hit-you-in-the-face kind of advertising, aren't nearly as effective, as these rely on people to walk or drive by them in order for them to work as intended.

Text message marketing works more effectively than other forms of advertising because of one reason: it goes to the people, rather than counting on the people to come to it. In addition, you can increase the number of your subscribers and bring your message to more and more people anytime, all the time.

Because people can be virtually anywhere in the world to receive your ad, you can reach a much larger number of people.

Email marketing is another form of Web marketing that is said to reach many people all over the world with one simple message, one simple email. However, any marketing expert will tell you that email marketing campaigns are rarely effective and are the modern version of mass letter, brochure, or flyer mail-outs that were once used by businesses.

But the problem is that people have so many filters on their email accounts because it's so easy to receive spam mail. Many consumers on email marketing lists don't even realize that they're on them and so the reason for the filters.

Not only is your email campaign then filtered out so that the consumer never actually sees it, but if they do, they are then angered that you are advertising to them when they don't want you to. *But, almost everybody reads their text messages.*

In fact, in the United States, 94% of cell phone users with text message capabilities on their phone have said that they read every text message that they receive.

Another one of the biggest benefits of text message marketing, especially to small businesses, is that it's inexpensive. You might even say that it's so incredibly cheap. If you hire a firm to send out your text messages for you, it could be as cheap as just two hundred dollars for one message to be sent to over one thousand customers. And of course, if you do it yourself it could be even less expensive. Depending on your own cell phone plan and the rates of your provider, it might even be free?

Compare that with a television or radio commercial, or even a newspaper ad, and you just can't get a lower price for reaching such a huge audience. For these two benefits alone, there is good reason to start your text message marketing campaign. There *are* even more benefits.

One of the less obvious benefits of text message marketing is that it's the preferred choice by the consumer. While this may not seem all that relevant to your business, think about when you've been bothered by an ad that you've seen.

Whether it's been too loud and in-your-face or you just didn't like the message that was sent, did it make you want to buy from that company? Were you inspired to use that product? Of course not. You'd probably rather just live without it than support the company behind it.

This is why using a marketing tactic that your customers support and enjoy is so important. When the person receives a text message, and that's their preferred way to find out about new products and sales, they are more open to receiving the message and more likely to buy the product. They are in a good mood.

Studies have shown that 39% of consumers in the United States prefer text message ads to any other kind – that's 76 million people. And the chances that your customers are somewhere in that mix is very good.

You can also play to your customer's sense of wanting to belong to something exclusive by creating offers and sales for only those that subscribe to your text messaging campaign.

You could advertise this on your website or in your store: "Want to know what sales and specials are only available to our text message subscribers? Sign up today!"

People want a good deal but more importantly, they want to know that they are getting something that others aren't, that they've found something that they can either reap the benefits of alone or, be the one to fill their friends in – which will benefit your profit margin the most.

Text message marketing is also a much more flexible form of advertising than others. If you plan a newspaper campaign, you have one chance to get the images right, get the text right, and run it for a certain number of days.

A television or radio commercial will deliver the same problems, with the exception that these are much more expensive.

However, with a text message marketing campaign, you can easily and quickly change it at any time you want, which makes it useful in so many other ways.

If you want to give your customers a heads up about a sale that's coming up at the end of the month, you can send them a text message or two to remind them of that. If you find that your restaurant is slow one night, you can send out a text message offering a free appetizer to the next ten customers that walk through the door. You can use text message marketing campaigns to increase future revenue, or to increase it instantly. Not a lot of other forms of marketing can boast the same benefit.

So text message marketing does a lot to boost your bottom line by communicating with customers and driving them to your business. This is one of the most obvious benefits of text message marketing, and undoubtedly **THE** most important benefit to your business.

But, there's another way that text message marketing helps increase your revenue; and it's one that many people, even business owners, aren't aware of, until they sign up for a program.

When an individual subscribes to a text message campaign, they are charged a certain fee from their mobile service provider usually this is a monthly fee.

However, without your messages the provider wouldn't have any messages to send and so, the provider will give you a certain percentage of the customer's monthly fee. Often this can be as high as 50% - that's a lot of revenue just for *starting* a campaign.

So How Does it Work Exactly?

So yes, a text message marketing campaign really has a lot of benefits for small business owners, and is very easy to set up. After all, you just set up an advertising campaign and then broadcast that out to a lot of different customers. It really is just as simple as that.

- But, where do you start?

- How do you just *create* a campaign?

- And where *exactly* are you supposed to get your customer subscription base from?

Yes, even though it's simple, there are still some details that you'll need to sort out.

And many of these details will require that you really think about what kind of campaign you want to run, and who exactly you're trying to reach.

Three Different Types of Text Message Marketing

The first thing you'll need to decide is which type of text message marketing you want to use. There are three different kinds. Which type you choose will depend on what you want your campaign to say, and how you want it to work.

Bulk Messaging Campaign

The most common type of campaign is the bulk messaging, or text blasting, type of campaign. This type of text message marketing is so common in fact, that when people refer to text message marketing, this is usually the type they are referring to. This is the simplest form of text message marketing, because it in a very basic form simply involves a broadcast text going out to a large number of people.

Within this text is whatever you want your customers to know, whether it's that there's a new sale, introducing new product or service, announcing a deadline or that you're holding an event. There should also be a call to action (like "Call us now!"). This helps reinforce the idea of the ad in the customer's mind and also prompts them to *do* something about what they just read.

This type of text message marketing is one of the simplest to run and, if you're going to be doing the entire campaign yourself, is probably the type of campaign you're going to choose. Any other type is going to require a pretty solid, maybe lengthy knowledge about servers, web applications, and databases. If you use a company to take care of the campaign for you, you may still be given software that you'll need to run whenever you want to launch your campaign. This software will contain the subscriber list, which will be the listing of numbers that the ad is being sent out to.

Whichever way you choose, with this type of text message campaign or any other, important is that the numbers on your subscriber list are authorized numbers. This means that the owner of the cell phone number has given permission that their number be on that list and it's OK to send ad messages. If not, that they have a way to opt-out of the subscription.

If you've ever received an email or text message with the line at the bottom, "If you choose to no longer receive this subscription, click here," with a link provided to take your name off the list, then you are probably very familiar with this concept.

There <u>must</u> be a way for people to opt out of the program. Not only will customers be annoyed with your text messages and turn away from your business rather than towards it, it's actually against the law in several countries to send out unsolicited texts.

Keyword Response Campaign

A keyword response campaign is the second most common type of text messaging campaign. This type of campaign only sends out a message when a user, or customer, has entered a keyword and it also works a little differently. Once the keyword has been entered, the person has automatically performed their call to action; essentially entering the keyword was all it took.

The message then tells them what will happen next. Your office may call them or they may receive an email, and always within a certain amount of time – people need to know when to expect your response.

These types of campaigns are especially good for organizations that need to coordinate things for different events, such as volunteer opportunities, ("We'll call you within 24 hours to set up your volunteer time,") or dentist /doctor appointments, ("It's time for your next check-up! The date we've reserved for you is January 1, we'll call to confirm within 24 hours").

This type of text message marketing campaign takes the most advantage of opening up the lines of communication between your business and your customer. You are not only actively encouraging that they call or *do* something, but you're also telling them that you care enough to call them, and when exactly you're going to do that.

But while this is definitely a great way to get everybody talking, it is extremely important to remember that <u>you need to follow up when you say you will follow up!</u>

If you can't call the customer back in six hours, don't say you will. If you know that you'll be able to call them back within the next 12 hours, say the next 24 to give yourself some wiggle room. Giving yourself too much time is much better than not having enough and needing to leave people hanging. This will actually backfire and make your campaign look very bad, because you already have not followed through with the promises you've made.

Smart Texting Campaign

Smart texting is the third main type of text message marketing campaign although it's much less common. Perhaps because it's a little more complicated and may require you to be a bit tech-savvy.

Smart texting campaigns work the same way that keyword-based campaigns do, but they take it one step further. After the call to action, the customer can then use their cell phone to get back to you. This may be in the form of another text, an email, attach a photo or file, or any number of things – all right from their cell phone.

Even more, once the customer has gotten back to you via their cell phone, you can then respond – all through the same campaign and the same program.

This type of text message marketing really takes the idea of using text message marketing to start a conversation, and takes it to the extreme, letting you have an entire conversation all with just a little software and one cell phone.

Once you've determined which type of campaign you want to run, you then have yet another decision to make: will you hire a commercial service provider or will you do it yourself?

To Leave it to Professionals,
or Do - It - Yourself?

Whenever there is a possibility that something could be done yourself and save you costs, people are always interested in knowing what it is and how to do it. And many times, they're even willing to give it a shot.

It's important to remember though, that in the case of text message marketing, it's not simply a matter of sitting down with your cell phone and punching in numbers. And unlike home remedies that you can DIY, you're probably not going to be able to set up an effective text message marketing campaign yourself with the tools that you have lying around your office.

And it may not even be the most cost-effective option, especially if you need to purchase new equipment such as servers and invest a lot of time in the campaign. That being said, it's definitely not *impossible* to set up and run a text message marketing campaign yourself.

The DIY Way

For those that are just starting out and don't really have all the techie know-how to set up servers and databases themselves, there are desktop clients available that are relatively easy to set up. For many you don't even need an Internet connection, just a supported phone line. These desktop versions often come with all the software you need to get started, including a subscription list, and complete instructions on how to install it and set it all up.

It's important to know that if you want to use a desktop version, that it's only really capable of handling a bulk messaging campaign. It's also important to understand that usually, desktop clients are only used for trial versions of campaigns or when you're just getting started in text message marketing.

When your campaigns get larger or you start using them more often, you'll need to upgrade to another type of campaign, which means more involvement and more complicated hardware and software.

The hardware and software that you'll need for more complicated campaigns are a GSM modem and SMS gateways. With these types of systems there is also a data storage compartment that you would also need to be familiar with.

These systems are extremely sensitive and have many different variables that all play a part in how they run and how efficiently they work. Because of that, they really do require someone that understands how servers work and has at least a basic knowledge of web applications and databases.

Once you've determined what kind of campaign you're going to run and that you have the know-how to do it, you then still need to iron a few more things out. One of those things is how you're going to compile your list of subscribers.

If you're running a desktop version of your software already contains a subscription list, this might not seem like a big deal. But there are things you can do to add to an existing list and if it didn't come with a list, you're going to need to start somewhere.

One place to look is through similar organizations or companies, which can be especially beneficial if you're linked to a charity or running a non-profit event. Contact these companies and find out if they have a newsletter or mail-out that you could advertise your subscription service in.

Some companies also have an existing subscription list of their own, which they may offer to sell to you. Make absolutely sure that if they offer, you make sure the people on the list have given permission for the company to sell their information. Otherwise, you are using unauthorized phone numbers and could face steep penalties for doing that.

Another way to get numbers on your subscription list is to straight out ask your customers for their mobile number. You can place a field for their number on small ballots inside your store, on flyers, on your own newsletters, or on any other printout that goes from you to your customer.

Of course, also make sure that there is a link to opt into the program somewhere on your website, so that online visitors will also have the chance to join there.

If you're ambitious and think that you have the knowledge required to set up a text message marketing campaign on your own, it can be a good idea and make you feel like you have more control.

But it's absolutely necessary that you ensure that you've fully researched your own legal responsibilities (and the consequences should you not meet them) and that you are fully aware of what makes a good campaign run. Otherwise, you could end up with a campaign that's poorly put together, and that will just make your company look bad in the eyes of your customers.

If you have no interest in, or don't think that you have the knowledge to, run a text message marketing campaign all by yourself, the good news is that there are thousands – yes, thousands – of mobile marketing companies that have dedicated themselves to getting your message out there to the crowds. How does that work? Much easier.

The Out-Sourcing Way

There is no need for feeling "inadequate" when you decide in hiring a mobile marketing company to run your text message marketing campaign. You are professional in your own field and text message marketing is a profession by itself. And, as mentioned before, hiring mobile marketing company could actually be less expensive and make your company look much better and more professional.

Either way, it will definitely be a whole lot easier. That's because *you* will still create the ad and *you* will still be the one that decides when and for how long your ad runs. The only difference is that you don't need to actually send the message out yourself and you don't need to worry about maintaining any of those servers and databases either. The only thing you really need to be concerned with, is finding the right mobile marketing company.

There's really only one way to start collecting names of mobile marketing companies, and that's by entering "mobile marketing companies, (your area)" into any search engine. Mobile marketing companies are Internet marketing companies, companies that live and breathe advertising on the Internet.

Because of this, they're going to have some of the most outstanding websites online to look at. You can go through them each one by one and start to get an idea of which ones might work best for you. This is a great way to immediately eliminate those that won't work, because they don't handle the type of campaign you want or you don't find their prices right, and move on. Once you have a few names of potential mobile marketing companies, you can then start calling around.

When you call around, arrange to set up a meeting between you and a representative. Try to meet the actual person that will be handling your campaign. It's fine if their supervisor or co-worker on the project will also be there, but make sure that the person who will actually be scheduling and sending your messages, is there for the meeting. This is the only way to ensure that you can accurately describe to them what your exact needs are.

When you meet with the mobile marketing company, make sure that you bring along a list of requirements that you need from them. Preparing this list ahead of time is a good idea because then you can just present them with all your needs at once, and you'll be sure that you didn't leave any out.

Include on the list things such as:

- How many subscribers you want to have,

- Whether you want to be able to divide up your subscription list into different categories, used for different campaigns,

- What kind of server space you require, if you know, and

- When and for how long you want your ad to run.

This list will give the marketing team a good idea of what's required of them, and if they'll be able to do it.

This meeting will give you a good indication about the different companies, and whether or not they're the right advertising team for you and your business. Still, you won't be able to make a final decision just yet.

Once you're finished with meeting all of the companies on your initial list, you can then narrow the list down to three that you liked the most. Contact all three again and ask each of them for a price quote. Make absolutely sure that when you do, you are getting a quote for the <u>same thing from each company.</u>

You don't want to get a quote for a smart texting type of campaign from one company and a quote for a bulk message campaign from another. The two are very different, and so are their prices. This will not be a good indication of whether or not the company's pricing is fair. You need to be comparing apples with apples.

Once the quotes have come in, you really do just need to consider everything you've learned up until this point - price *and* more – and decide on which company you think will be best for your text message marketing campaign.

Remember that you need a company that will provide you with everything you need, and that you feel comfortable with, and that brings it all for an affordable price. So, what should that be?

The Cost of Text Message Marketing Campaigns

Text message marketing is undoubtedly one of the cheapest forms of advertising that you could invest in, and it's not even all that much of an "investment" as it is an "expense," that's how little it costs. The cost of bulk messages is by far the cheapest; but this too is good news seeing as how this is the most popular form of text messaging.

Mobile marketing companies will generally have a one-time set-up fee that can vary greatly, but usually starts at around $75 - $299. In addition to this, you will then need to pay a fee for the messages that are sent out.

The minimum amount of messages you can buy is usually somewhere around 500 a month, for about $50 - $100, while you can purchase as many as 10,000 messages a month for a costlier price of around $800 - $1,000. You can also of course, choose to buy even more messages for that, for an even higher price.

Many people who are concerned with the price of text message marketing are also concerned with how much it costs their customers to receive their text messages.

After all, if your customers have to pay just to see your ad, this will also leave a sour taste in their mouth regarding your company, won't it? Well first, remember that they have opted in and so, there is a benefit to them for signing up and they did know about that fee when they opted in. But still yes, they may be charged a fee from their mobile service provider for receiving your text messages. Because there are so many different mobile carriers, it's impossible to tell how much one will be charged for receiving a message on their cell phone.

If you're concerned about it, or want to be able to tell your customers about it when they opt in for the program, you can also contact major carriers in your area and ask them what their rates are. Many also have unlimited plans.

That being said, text messaging is quickly becoming the main form of communication for many people – even more than actual phone calls from cell phones.

Carriers can also provide text messaging to their customers at very little cost to them, and it's also much cheaper than providing cellular service for phone calls. Because of these two factors combined, many carriers are now offering free unlimited text messaging to their clients, which means you can tell your customers it's not costing them a thing to opt into your program.

The Wording of a Mobile Marketing Campaign

Now that you know what kind of campaign you want, how to do it yourself or hire a mobile marketing company, and a little bit about pricing a text messaging campaign, it's then time to think about the actual ad you are going to use in your campaign.

The actual words in your campaign are the most important part. After all, it doesn't really matter how well you execute a campaign if, in the end, the finished ad is confusing or irrelevant to the readers. And while we've already touched on a few things you should consider when it comes to the wording of your text message ad, such as including a call to action, there are also a few other things that you'll want to have in mind.

The first is that you will only have 160 characters – that's *characters*, not *words*. Twitter messages are up to 140 characters long, just for comparison.

And while this may sound like a lot, it's really not. That means that you have a very short amount of time to get a very important message across to your customers. This is not the time to delve into your company's history, it's the time to tell your customers why you're there and what you have to offer to them.

It's now time to make them want to find out more, and to become interested in your product. Get in any of the most important information first such as your phone number, the promotion code they need, or when the sale is running. Then include your call to action. You'll probably be surprised that by the time that is done, you're almost at your character limit – and you might even have to cut what you have, down to proper size.

Always remember to include the word "exclusive" on it somewhere, whether it be "an exclusive text offer", "for our exclusive customers," or something else along those lines.

Although people might learn that they'll receive exclusive offers when they first sign up for your program, they may forget this somewhere along the way, and it's always a good thing to remind them of it.

This one may sound obvious, but include the name of your company somewhere within that 160 characters. Often times a text message will be sent out and only your ad appears, without your company's name or a link to your website.

If your name isn't mentioned somewhere within the ad, your customers will receive an ad, but they won't know where to go, who to call, or what to do. And then it doesn't matter how well you planned your marketing campaign, how well it was executed, or how powerful the rest of the words are. If your customer doesn't know what to do after all of that, your ad is entirely useless.

Conclusion

There is a reason that text message marketing is becoming the most popular form of advertising for big and small businesses alike – they have a lot of benefits and sales results.

And in addition to that, they're incredibly easy to pull off.

Like any other marketing campaign, they do have their own issues that need to be considered and details that need to be ironed out.

But they still don't require near the thought or time other types of campaigns do, and they certainly reap many more benefits. In the end though, a well thought out text messaging marketing plan might just be the best one you'll ever have.

Next Steps

Thank you again for investing your time and money in this informational report. We hope that you found it useful and it has given you the information you needed to help you better understand the most important things you should know before starting your mobile marketing campaigns.

If you would like additional assistance, please contact us at:

dm@cyconsocialmedia.com

Tel: 281.891.3111

About the Author

Duke Morris is President of
CyCon Consulting LLC, a
social media marketing
consulting firm.

CyCon Consulting specializes in working with small and very
small businesses, helping them optimize their online marketing
presence and brand recognition through social media sites,
videos, blogs and mobile marketing platforms.

CyCon Consulting, LLC

www.cyconsocialmedia.com

www.ingramcontent.com/pod-product-compliance
Lightning Source LLC
Chambersburg PA
CBHW071555170526
45166CB00004B/1688